BLUEROSE PUBLISHERS
India | U.K.

Copyright © Rohan Khanna 2024

All rights reserved by author. No part of this publication may be reproduced, stored in a retrieval system or transmitted in any form or by any means, electronic, mechanical, photocopying, recording or otherwise, without the prior permission of the author. Although every precaution has been taken to verify the accuracy of the information contained herein, the publisher assumes no responsibility for any errors or omissions. No liability is assumed for damages that may result from the use of information contained within.

BlueRose Publishers takes no responsibility for any damages, losses, or liabilities that may arise from the use or misuse of the information, products, or services provided in this publication.

For permissions requests or inquiries regarding this publication, please contact:

BLUEROSE PUBLISHERS
www.BlueRoseONE.com
info@bluerosepublishers.com
+91 8882 898 898
+4407342408967

ISBN: 978-93-6452-588-6

First Edition: August 2024

To the Australian rebels and our late night 'bakchodi sessions' in New Jersey. Thank you for the inspiration — This book is my ode to you.

Cheers,
Dr. R

Once upon a time
On a cold winter night

Class was in session
&

The teacher became
the student

As children, we have all learned some version of ABCD

As adults, sometimes it's important to go back to school

 APPLE

b BADA APPLE

 CHOTA APPLE

 DOBARA APPLE

 EK AUR APPLE

F FIR SE APPLE

 GAJAB BHAI, EK AUR APPLE

 HARAMI APPLE

 IDHAR DE APPLE

 JUNGLI APPLE

 KALA APPLE

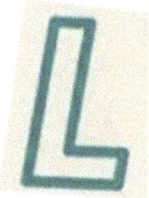 L PE, TERA APPLE

 NIKAMMA APPLE

 PHATI KA APPLE

 Q CHAHIYE APPLE

 RAKH LE TU APPLE

T

TERI GAND MAI
DALU 12 APPLE

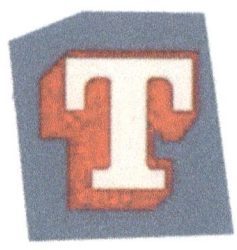

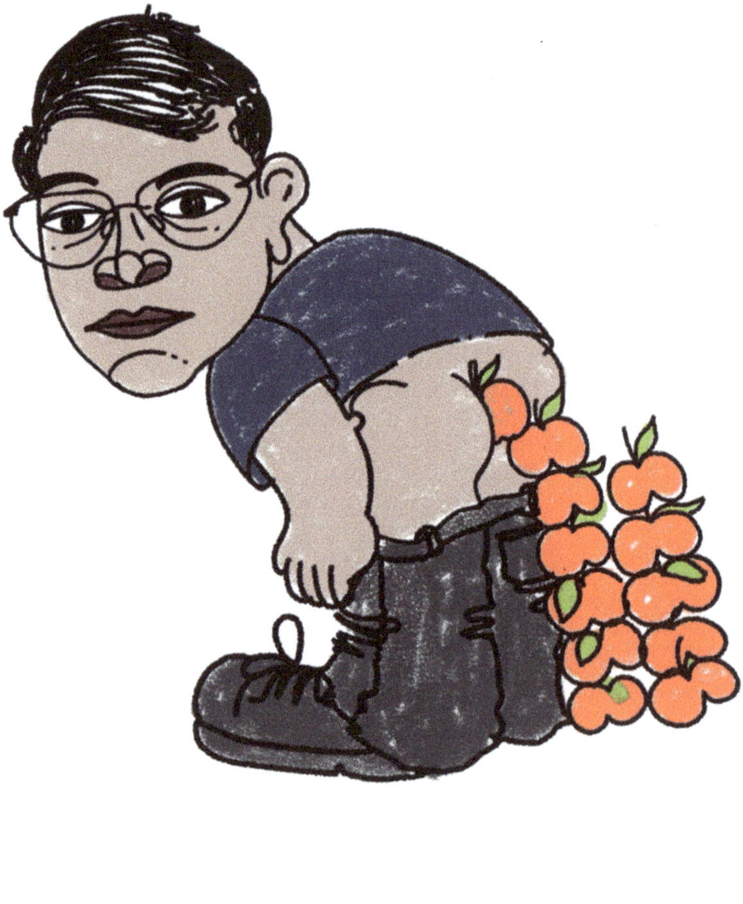

ULTA APPLE

 VIAGRA WALA APPLE

 WAHA LELE APPLE

 X RATED APPLE

ZIDD NA KAR, AB GAND MEIN DAAL LE APPLE

"An apple a day
Keeps the doctor away"

Butttt......

If the nurse is cute,
fuck the fruit

"He had me in love at F, never got to z".

— The wife

"He is somewhat useful at work but irreplaceable at parties"

— The boss

"Woof-woof, fuckin brilliant"

— The dog

The author is a middle aged dog dad trying to stay funny. Sometimes, just sometimes, he comes up with shit that leaves people in stitches. This is the "fruit" of one such time.

New York Times BESTSELLER

www.ingramcontent.com/pod-product-compliance
Lightning Source LLC
LaVergne TN
LVHW061530070526
838199LV00010B/445